The Darkest Day

The Darkest Day

By Alaric Cabiling

Praenomen Press
Richmond, Virginia

ISBN: 978-0-615-24688-8

Praenomen Press
Richmond, Virginia

To my parents, Nimfa and Adelino, who continually teach me that unconditional love conquers all.

Contents

Come In

You come and go like the wind.

The guests come and go

as they please.

Emasculating eyes ravage

the moment. Chandeliers.

Bottles of wine.

Curious misgivings.

Sprawling

relentless surrender,

spiraling beyond the naked eye.

Hearts blossom from within.

Curious that you have come,

but indeed,

the night is young, so to you I say, come in.

You come and go like the nightsky.

The Seine sparkling

in the moonshine. Ravenous

delight. Momentous in the day.

Monumental in the night.

The dinner guests are up

and about and as one may

attest, litanies

are spread, canticles

are sung,

and oh, the night is young.
But where, oh where,
to begin?
Curious that you seem…
too keen to drift away as though
your countenance were but
a dream, but to you I say,
come in.

The words will mark their sheltered
moments in the sun. But for now,
the dreams wearily depart
and oh, the night is young.
The cordial heat rises
with the ocean's tide. Sprawling
relentless surrender,
spiraling beyond the naked eye.

Eternity

We hold fast the fire that bestills the night.
The slow fire that smolders in the heart
by day is the same slow flame
that churns throughout the dark.
Hence, desire has a name.

We fasten the memory of an event
much the same way. We take
its wings and wrap them around
from behind to hinder flight.
We place memory in a cage.

We rummage through the dark closets
of life and only plunder in vain.
We take an antiquated rhyme
and chime only memories which thus
remain. Hence, the tourniquet of time.

We ponder the quandary of immortality
in but a breath. That emancipation
is merely a manumission
of the flesh. With the fire that burns,
hence eternity. With freedom,
hence, the vigil of death.

The End of Innocence

Somewhere, somehow, I must have imagined

that the vision of the world was that

of a sparkling white. Everything

in the world was iridescent to the naked eye.

An incandescence at birth, an afterglow

at the demise of the world. Light laid no remorse

as it held its claim and everything was marked

by a shimmering devoid of shadow.

Light filled every fissure, and every pillar

and every fixture glimmered with gold.

Even in the night sky,

everything sparkled like jade. And in the dawn's

first light, darkness was but the only thing

that would fade away.

Innocence ruled the day. Its color was white.

Everything reveals itself in time, I supposed, or so

I hoped. The great mystery, that is, the origin

of time states itself quite matter-of-factly

in almost everything from the blue sky

to the deep blue sea. Both are expanses

that are deemed to represent the infinite.

Eternity in our very midst.

The shore. The sky. Insurmountable. Inconceivable.

They simply are. And are we artifacts

of their existence? Catalogs or chronicles

of their resilience? Marked only by our frailty

and temporality in every essence.

Contemplative in the meager form of an I, me or you.

It was the span of immortality. Its color was blue.

Some time had passed and something else

came to my attention. Light travels at such

a speed as to render it impossible to chart

with the naked eye. There was

something else much slower than this.

It diffuses in all directions and consumes

the heart's most modest intentions.

It burns through the damp drapes of summer and climbs

the frames and descends the pillars. Soon,

the wood planks are torn asunder and out

it goes into the fields of solace, spelling doom

as quickly as it had spread.

Only time can tell when such a maturation awaits

such machinations.

It was the light of desire. Its color was red.

And then darkness fell upon the world. Light flashed

from out the gloom and everything was desolate.

Everything seemed antiquated, or the others,

obsolete. There was death and there was depravation.

There was malady and apprehension. Hope had fled.

Shards of light broke through the shutters by day

and in the night darkness engulfed the world like

an open grave.   Nothing shimmered. None

but the ghosts of memory.

The fires burned and black smoke covered

the earth. I looked up and there was not

an absence of profundity in the world. This held

sway. But all of wonderment would not return.

The world as it once was known would not come back.

Hence this knowledge has been all I've ever known.

Its color is black.

Little Wings On a Heart's Longing

Pull a string on a heart's lyre
  and hear it sing.
Is love truly the antecedent
to all things?
Memoirs in the wind.
A heart's longing on little wings.
A dew drop waiting on a blade
  of grass. A loved one's
    last wave on the oceans
of chance. A wind rustling
through the trees, and
one thinking,
  how free it would feel
    to fly away and yet
never truly leave.
Love drifts in its own expanse.
And as the sun sets and a tint of gold
covers the horizon's steamy edge,
love just as easily
  fades into the past.
What predicates the search for this?
This incalculable cry.
This incongruous need.
To pull a string on a heart's lyre
and be ravaged by the pangs
of desire.
To hence, become one with the fire.

Subliminal

Wakefulness stirs something innate at its earliest.

Something struggling to break onto
the surface of the lake sees
the rippling light growing larger beyond it.

Something that relinquishes something else and takes
hold of the wind at its most preemptive.

Something in the sky that knows that the rain
must fall and never pauses to wonder why
the clouds condense, the steam gathers
into such curlicues of mist.

You open your eyes at the scenery that greets you—
a moment's forestalling of memory
soon comes to an end, lest
a reprise awaits you.

You flutter your eyes to disperse the shadows,
to gather the light. The empty chairs look vacuous
and bare. You cradle your closed eyes in
your sunken hands. Your lips trace
the ghost of a smile. Fissures in the stillness
don't seem quite as immense. Time, as it
mostly does, whittles by.

Leviathan of Night

Will the sad crows caw at the dawn's early light?
The moon is a man's sad face high up
in the darkness.
Will you come outside?

The trains rumble along the tracks predestined for
aridness.
You can hear the dreams rushing
into the night's plethora
of dreamers. The winds cease and the rivers are still.

Wires connect multiple worlds. As do the bridges.
At the fountain square, in the very
center of sadness, music
swirls. Hearts flare. Shadows converge.

What is in place of the dream within the dreamless?
The astute awareness that relays
its foreboding in the stillness,
that allows your vigilance to patiently remain, and is ever
aware

that nothing is in vain. Wings of whimsicality are flung
aside as fanciful wings are meant for flying.
Now then,

the dreams are out of their wombs and the dreams are
dying.
Come out. Come out. Come out of your hiding.

Cedar Drive

Sitting outside a lonely house

on Cedar Drive

The tall trees stand steadfast

in the cool evening breeze

of a warm summer's night.

This night is a severance from the days.

I remember the rain pouring down

upon a land I once called

home

far, far away.

I recall crowds of people

with umbrellas and taxi cabs and the branches

of trees swaying with the monsoon winds

and the bad traffic on narrow

broken streets.

I remember puddles of rain

I would skip over with my shiny black shoes

carrying a notebook filled with little dreams

and little portals onto a bridge over a creek

I mockingly called the ridge of escape.

I recall dreams dancing to the drumming

of disarray.   Standing alone in a theater

called the Gourge with the lights slowly dying

and a piano at center stage humming its own

hymn of dismay with a moonlit serenade.

I remember walking out at night

with the westerly winds beckoning to take

me to a place east of Eden. The dark clouds gathering

in the sky and the books in my arms with wings

meant to fly…

Sitting alone on steps made of stone.

The lonely house on Cedar Drive that was never home.

Taking life a day at a time with the easterly winds

beckoning

to take me back to a land that was never mine

and singing la de dah, come what may.

This night marks an end of old ways.

Waiting For the Dark

Where we are

we can no longer ascertain

the rays of light that dwindle with the stars

at dawn

from the drowning inundations of dusk.

All the lighthouses that beckon forsaken ships

drawn to forsaken treasures

merely illuminate the dark.

We float like rafts

in the open tide (shunned when all words

Were spoken out of pride - futile attempts

To reconcile a breath from out its breast

Severed from its heart),

satellites launched with flailing premonitions

to the sun,

the tender courtship of death

beyond the knowledge of its bride -

recrimination unto self.

We are indignant unto death the moment

we blatantly disavow life…who knows where we are..

where we are now…

we can't imagine what the bottom will be like.

Ode to Abdication

Times change. Cold dark nights
relinquish themselves
willingly to the days.
Dry gravel roads stretching
onwards for miles and miles
still find their eyes affixed heavenward
in search of rain.

Sunless skies, starless nights, reckless schemes
superimposed upon a chance to glorify
the meanderingly obscene,
or perhaps,
the abdication of a dance,
the blueprints of a master plan inexplicably
left to chance,
the dying desiderata of a dream.

How else will a man celebrate
the unfastening of his mortal chains
than to revel in the ardor
of his feverish relapse? As though
there were nothing more to be gained.
The more things change, the more
they stay the same?
Lampposts luminescent on cobblestone

walkways present an endless parody
of a wintry night's starless haze.
The doves are silent.

Clouds hover above us just enough
so steam rising from open cisterns gathers
quietly in the sky.
The light antiquates the darkness. Even
in the daytime the surreal tends
to superimpose upon the sublime.
Times change. Perhaps, we've forgotten.
Everything evolves as it remains.

Ode to Emptiness

Emptiness is like a fire that scorches the overgrown hills
of sorrow. It desecrates its temple. It chars
every single remnant of an ideal.

It snares the only sanctity in the sufferance of sorrow.
It lays desolate its every validity. It is
the culmination in the progress of frailty.

Soon the skies will have nothing below them.
Everything will have retreated into
the subterranean. The oceans

of the earth will awash every desolation.
Every promise will have its apt negation.
Every betrayal will likewise end with a promise

negated. The death of the cycle. The ruination.
The unspeakable alienation. The emptiness.
Sorrow overruns the stillness.

Desperation does its part. If madness does not descend,
emptiness is its only consequence.
Emptiness, it is said, is the only
true apocalypse of the heart.

Hearts Run Dry

We have our hearts and our hearts
      have run dry.

We have our chains and all that is left
  of the day is all
      that remains.

We have the tranquil days
      and the tranquil nights.

We have dreams that deem to merely
  fade away. As do
      all dreams.

Nothing ever stays the same.

We've had the years and still
      the years go by.

We've had the snow and the rain. We've
  had the summer nights
      that still remain.

We've had the aura noir's nomadic
      spangles of light.

We've had bright yellow tips of delight

  burning atop smudges

    of blue desire.

Nothing ever solely fades in but a night.

Alone in Death

Can't you discern a man who is close to death?
Why the head down?
In this defiance I breathe my last breath
in the breadth of the circumstance.
I would embark upon the apocalypse if its genesis
would mean my death.
Life has amounted to little or no significance left.

Life was in itself, the funeral pall enough.
Its length is the extent of the season.
Its width is the breadth of reason.
Why come with head down?
Earthly souls have been cast in the sorrows
of time. In my death, lamentation
has become an aberration
of the mind.
There are no mourners left.

Upon the raveling sea, I will be reborne
in kind. Eyes cast upon the ocean's
tide will depose the banks
of eternity. What little is known
of the intricacy sown within the weave
of immortality isn't one's to atone.
Why come then, when you

come alone? In my death, the omega
is much the alpha bereft. There
weren't others then. There are no others
left.

The Damnable Art

A voice calls out. I hear a piano
  softly playing.
Some say that I do not know how
to listen. And some,
on the other hand,
say that it's all I ever
really do.

All in the midst of being a mute.

Some talk, talk,
until the wary cliché catches them napping,
  'til there is nothing more to be said
and still,
the fine art, now damned and disfigured,
is all but dying.
Talk, talk.
The rite of rambling, the meat of defeat,
The wine of whining.
I wouldn't know how to listen
to such talk…there stems the accusation
and therein too lies the question –
If some people were to talk,
and some to listen,

and some to balk at the very notion

that some people do nothing

but talk, talk, talk,

then who is to suffer the thought

of people who do nothing but

talk lament of people

who do nothing but listen, listen,

listen?

Wanting

It angers me to want something. Something unbecoming
of me. Such a thing aroused from a sadness
at the nothingness of a state of being.
That I must inherit the essence
of such a thing that is
to append to
my life,

that is to enrich it in a certain way, somehow makes a mockery
at its own insistence. Of wanting, longing for
something more in the needling heat
of passion, of more than just
the spirit of existence,
that is to yearn
for more

than life itself. Though I am helpless to it, swayed into the riptide
and pulled down into the undertow of life at the very notion
that I must adjunct to myself, the very spirit of desire
that beguiles me in essence to
devour myself. Something.
Someone. Anything.
Everything.

The wanting for more, more than that which can bewilder the eye,

subdue the heart's innermost desire, crave the warmth of the

fire and its own inevitable undoing. More than

the mere monotony of living. Is it folly

for such a man who has not

lived to hold contempt

for such things

unknown to him? For a man to shun a dream and want nothing.

Nothing in exchange for the nothingness within. The

soliloquy spoken without promise. Nothing

more than this. This earth. This

flaccid rebirth. This charred

bit of coal. This

solitary soul.

Winter of Your Year

The hearth is a grave of stone, mortar,
sweating rock. The fires
that once burned are forever gone.

One man says to me, his days have been
forever filled with the same
ashen days and pallid nights
of late, but wait,
they're back. No, here they are,
waiting still.

The morning air has been cold and damp.
Lovers flee their tender traps.
The vapor's weight hangs in the density
of mist.

The heart is a grave of grime and dust.
Oh weep! Weep, for the heart
if you must.

No sooner than when the thought entrances,
the lights go out. The spirit leaves
the vigil of its senses.

One man says to me, the days have been

darker as of late, the nights

have forever been the same,

but wait, they're here.

They truncate. They gravitate.

Everywhere, a silence drifts in the miasmal

air. Outside, the clouds condense.

Everything is waiting for something

to happen. The chairs

are empty. The tables

are set.

Sara

Sara thinks the world could fade away
at any given moment. Her
long brown hair flows
upon her shoulders and long slender
fingers glide reproachingly on
the carpet.
Her right hand extends past
the curve of her breast and she
slowly reaches out, as if to claw
her way out of a well, and her
hand stretches out to feel
the warm rays of the ominous
sunset that drew her here,
as have the others who have come,
but of course, within her beating heart
lies a less sinister intent. Less
than lying on the beach for hours
watching beautiful women walk by,
less than staring at lifeguards
for hours despite the burn of the sun
tenderly dissolving the skin
on their arms. Her cabin
holds an ominous view; and she walks
by the water daily, letting
the surf engulf her smooth

ankles, welcoming her
as though she would never return.
But not today.
Sara lies alone in the bedroom of her cabin;
she thinks the world has come of age.
She is in reach of her phone as
she stretches far across where she lays
and angrily pushes it away.

Sara cannot recall a lovelier summer's day.
The tide's soft gentle music rises
within her; the soft amber twilight rays
seem to seductively outlay a pathway
to the open skies. Sometimes she wonders
what it must be like to walk into the waters
with one of her former lovers, as she
has never done so, to this day.
She's been alone for years and only recalls
the ungainly romances that only
further her darkest fears. She has
never known true love, and has given up
on climbing its most elusive staircase
ascending into the stars.
She thinks about a boy she was once
very enamored with and struggles
to hold mightily onto the ropes
fastened around her deepest

intentions. Why would she mourn

for him, she wondered.

He never wanted her.

Sara pulls from deep inside of her,

The bravest convictions. She has her

demons spread out before her,

and as she looks up at the window

just above her bed, a ray of light

bestows the blessing she seeks

for this mightiest of missions.

Sara clutches at her robe and recalls

her family and friends and all

the people she's come to know, and

for a while a sadness rises to the

peak of the trough, and falls as it

does time and time and again. Sara thinks

of the warm ray of light and at the instant

she does,

she thinks she might be blessed.

Sleep to Dream

When once a flash of light sweeps across
a thundering sky…

When once a blossoming flower relents
to such ordinations of the clime…

When once the weary eye bears the cloak
of wind, and yet struggles
to fervidly deny such whims…

I longed to dream of life – the somewhat stabbing transfixion
of the mind…the knowledge bleeding from the wounds
corrupted by time…but no,
I sleep to dream of death – the tantalizing temporal awareness
subjugating the mind…and I awaken with the realization
of what it is that I have cradled in bed like a lover
in the night – the shriveling tissues of the wanton truth:
my own precarious demise.

When once the ashen sky dons the pallid
soul within…

When once the nothingness dreams of its filling,
and the fullness craves for the nothingness
therein…

What then is there to stop repudiation?
One braves the slow tidal descent into somnolence,
sweet immortal cessation,
sown intrinsically into the notion of tranquility
begotten of eternal rest.
The tranquility you constructed. . .
to fondly recall feeling nothing,
the anticipation of an old belonging,
leaping, like a quagmire redundancy, over a gap in the
bridge…and falling,
falling,
falling ecstatically into the wind.

Exile On Earth

1. You.

Where are all the transcripts on your desk?

And the manuscripts you have yet

To review? The odds

are insurmountable. A verve,

a line, a misspelled word.

Immeasurable.

Immense.

The parodies are endless. The

parallels, inscrutable.

But what was that word we always playfully

imagined? Pondered the syllogism

of such a word?

Potential.

You race off with your latte and your coat

ad make off to the nearest café, as if,

you needed any more of it.

But you could never argue that

against yourself anyway.

2. Me

The wintry years seem over at least.

Everything seems

to be dampened by an air of the funereal.
I take my car and drive north of the city;
there, I'll find a museum,
a favorite library,
and a much-loved café with a featured
espresso of the week that
has jovially become routine.
However inconsequentially.
However late.
I'll reach my destination,
take my pocket planner,
admire the filigree
while I walk happily in the rain.

3. Exile.

The well is dry.
The rocks slit my hands with their jagged
edges. The chains of hope
that dangle above
are beyond my reach.
The moon is overseer of the scheme.
Already, I've known
its undulations quite
pervasively.
As if I were to comprehend
the meaning of all this.

Dust will fill the entirety

of this hole in the earth,

and so will the secrets

of the world go along

with it.

As if my life

had any space

to fill…

the semantics of

a word.

The white spaces of a blank page.

The sad circumstances of the world.

4. Betrayal.

Some of the days we had spent working

together would culminate in the same event.

I'd clear my desk and drop

by your office at the end

of the day and you'd

look up and nod in agreement.

We'd walk out and step into your car

and the silence would fall

and the well-guarded pupils of your eyes

would flutter to welcome

the light. You'd push a button

and the sounds of a saxophone

would tell the tales

of a million secrets

you never lent,

the sad rules you never bent,

the torrid, broken tears you never wept

and you would turn to me and smile.

Sometimes I actually don't miss you as much.

I suppose it feels a little odd…a thought

migrates an emotion to my heart that blisters with

the irrational sense of betrayal of having ceased,

even just for a time,

the mourning of a friendship long gone.

Going Unnoticed

A road presents a curious tryst. They extend
from point A to point B to a point C
and so on. Multitudinous
perhaps, even more so, infinite.

They are a jarring labyrinth of turns and twists.
You find yourself on one such as that
this very minute, unaware
of such peculiar details – a streetlamp,

a mailbox, a billboard, and so
forth. The language of love
is so distinct. This, shelters all things
unapparent. You fumble

with a map and identify the path
you've taken. You take a sip
from your cup. The trunk of your car
presents an allegory of all things

forsaken, for whatever reason you
hold on to them. Perhaps
forlorn of everything else of any
conceivable dimensions,

they are all you have left.
You take an exit off the interstate
and you remember someone vaguely.
Disconnected, you fail to check

the rear-view mirror at that very instant
you recollect, as if there was nothing
there, a shard of glass to entomb
the past in the present.

Purpose of Profound Volition

It is perhaps

the only point worthy of presumption…this notion

that I could've

    or would've otherwise

impaired the logic

of a most

perilous

    infraction of time for such

a purpose unknown

to a most profound volition.

I'd march straight

into the velveteen dampness

of the drapes that signal the ascent

into your apartment high

    above the streets.

With the aging books

antiquating silently amongst

themselves,

with the bookends corroding

compliantly upon the shelves,

    the days go fairly unnoticed

as if time itself

were shedding its own persistent self

    in runnels.

And most nights find you gone,

somewhere,
  armed with the impetus of subtle implication,
marking the end of a journey with an afterthought
in lieu
  of an ideation.

These are the days.
Amidst the noise, you can hear
  the sound
of a decaying city's
        dead dreams
fermenting quietly in the heat.
Notions
squander conundrums amidst
  the foray.
You could have come anytime, could you not have?
but,
  you did not.
And thus veneration templates
  the semblance
        of a plot. This,
        this wanton attempt
of an adherence of thought,
this
  undoing of a hex stamped blatantly
upon the guise of Salem's lot,
this truant

defiance of time.

This lost absolution called love.

These things we either

conceal

or we vaguely

ponder upon whimsy with a 'would I?'

or 'would I not have?'

uttering line

after inconsequential line.

But these things we cannot deny.

Death is the inevitable end to a journey.

The only true darkness I

can see

is the memory

of an event

and the irresolution of one's incapacity

to undo it.

I will not mark

the memory with a tactile seasonality

of a 'would I?'

or 'would I not?,' quite

perfunctorily

with a question…as if to abash

with the mere asking.

I would tell you, I would.

Indeed I would.

Your window is the darkest of all

the others visible from below.

Noises erupt

  quite nonchalantly

from…

everywhere, I suppose.

Its far quieter where you are.

These are the days.

These days find you proud.

The hustle and bustle never

quite dissipates. Silence imbues

the longing. The nights cover the city's naked limbs

quite affably as would

  a burial shroud.

Return to Desolation

I came as quickly as the winds of fate

could take me. Pale December

has disheveled the ghost

of autumn. And now,

the carrion of summer is all that remains

of the once bountiful season. As

quickly as this has changed,

so too did the news

of your passing arrive. And so here

I make my way through the streets

of Bedlam. Eternity

once marked its incipience upon

the mountains of the foreground. Time

trickles in teardrops falling

from the fountain

square. The townsmen seemingly

drift like ghosts of the nigh.

And I, though no stranger

seem unwelcome. The streetlamps seem

to yield expectantly, as the mists

of the ether slowly descend

from the yonder sky.

I arrive at your apartment, turn on the light,

and I watch as the shadows

slowly retreat as far as

what is beyond their reach. Cardboard boxes

and tattered covers. Tongues of fire

in manifold clusters. It is only

my specter that vacillates the emptiness

and gathers round the patches

of darkness and slowly speaks

to the gaps,

the fissures, the naked fixtures.

There is much to consider of someone

you've barely known and sometime loved.

How little there is to examine

fully when one is living. How great it is,

a quandary to be pondered when one

is gone. Just as your remains once

bristled with the breath of folly,

the dreams have departed the very objects

that once provided them with scenery.

With color. With a language

of fluency. There,

in the corner, are some bookshelves. A lamp,

an antique table, old leather furniture,

pictures that merely stare. None,

may be so aware that life

once gave credence to chaos,

and that your living once sparked

relevance to a conglomeration of objects

at random and which thusly return to a fate

wherein they once had flourished.

Only the ghost of memory

to rekindle what has thus diminished.

In your bedroom, I peer out the window.

The vacant air seems fitting.

The empty streets wear desolation well.

I sit on your unmade bed and wonder,

Try to comprehend the incomprehensible.

 It seems that

they left this room the same. All the rest, they've

draped with sheer covers. I gaze

around me. I find my own reflection

in the mirror. How quickly,

I thought, does the solitary tide

turn in the midst of eternity.

The bare sheet is cold and baffling.

I trace the outline of an arm

along its labyrinth-like undulations.

There is more than the mere prevalence

of cold air and obscurity settled

amongst the artifacts of memory.

Someone is here. Someone is watching.

Sadness Is

Sadness is a friend.

Sadness comes and sadness goes.

It beckons like a lover

in your bed. It looms. It sates

the hunger. Joy relentlessly

departs. Sadness relentlessly surrenders.

Sadness is only mercurial

to the heart. Sadness seeks

to make amends.

Sadness never truly ends.

Sadness is the instigator.

Sadness embodies solitary awareness.

Sadness is the experimental stage.

Sadness is the grave. Sadness

is Ophelia. It is both impulse

and stimulus. It is rancor.

It is quiescence.

Emptiness is its remains.

Sadness pacifies. Sadness placates.

Sadness never seeks to nullify.

Sadness merely takes its place.

Sadness is the face

of life. Sadness is more

than mere melancholy. Sadness

reaps the gain of strife.

Sadness goes. Sadness stays.

Sadness resonates in the breath

of folly. Sadness rarely

departs without delay.

It is the darkness of night.

It is the light of day.

It is the mist in the ambiguity

of twilight. Sadness is the flesh

of the fire. Sadness is the stain

of sin. Sadness is desire.

Sadness is within.

Augury

Inauspicious tomorrow.
Precious pain. Precious gift.
Seasons of sorrow adrift.

Disinterred.
The desecrated earth.
The dark firmament. Ashen sky.
Afterbirth.

Winds of Windsor.
Wings of death. The midnight
burns of lamentation.
The tombs relent.

The dead amongst
the living dwell. Eyes cast.
Hearts swell. Sir Mordred
draws his horrid lance.

At a glance, all is well.
Memento Mori.
Memories fleeting. Wings beating
within a glass.

Winds of change.

Winds of chance. Lightning

falls upon the land.

Circumstance.

Infernale

My incapacity to love is a startling fact.

Desire, as I have said in the past,

is a libidinous red.

The granite heart is instead,

ashen grey within my chest.

I have been remarked to be cold, to this effect.

I touch a flower and the vim and vitality

siphon from out its withering stem.

It is at once, one with the ground

upon the touch of death.

It spreads at the searing speed of sound.

From out my lips, a poem mouths out

its own unwillingness to exist.

It hangs in the corpus delicti of the moment.

A ghost in the mist. A frivolous fact

sailing on a ship without a mast.

The curve of a smile, needless to resist,

is sometimes worth the while.

Upon meeting at last, there exudes

from the smile an unsavory rasp befitting

The Belial. At once, an eternal smile

is one of denial. One aghast!

Love Eternal

Love eternal.
Malleable to the touch.
Recumbent to the nigh.
Flesh of the fire.

Love eternal.
Transcendental thought.
Spirit come alive.
Degradation of desire.

Love tranquil.
Serenity of supple warmth.
Anguish of anticipation.
Inanity of the heart.

Love morbid.
Committal of misfortune.
Ill of the intrinsic.
Fortress of dissolution.

Love benign.
Pliant as the vine.
Vagabond of time.
Precursory presumption.

Love eternal.

Continuity of strife.

Bestiality of breath.

Love eternal. Vicissitude of death.

Strolling Along the Seine

The boardwalks are vacant. The museums
are empty. The tennis courts are empty
as well. It is not
a night for such extravagances. In any case,
it's far too late. I stroll down the Seine
at half past ten in the evening
and the faint glimmer shimmering on the ebony surface
of the water is reminiscent to that of the moonlight
shining down on a secluded lake.

How strange it is to walk parallel
to the ebbing water. Softly and gently it flows
beyond me. I hear the faint sound of a piano
playing, and the music that breathes fitfully
to the river's movement mimics my own
short jaunt with destiny. In the night,
the path is well-lit, and once
or maybe twice a night, a traveller such as I
finds another. We nod at each other.
We smile. We look away.
This is the magic of the river.
It bears no answers.
It merely reminds us of the hereafter.
The infinite in all things. That there is always
an anecdote and also, a new beginning.

We are strangers seeking the same.

I turn at the last stop and I always
look back. Every so often desperation drives
me to its eager hands.
I see the same tumult in someone walking by.
We glance. We look away.
No words need betray the silence.
We are mimes in the darkness.
We are all children of chance.

Sweet Misery

Sweet misery, the nights won't
burn long before the fervent
nights go cold.
The midnight oil won't cease to fuel
the fire before the heart's
forlorn passion will cease to
nourish the flame.

Sweet misery, the docks won't
end the tides' relentless
journeys amongst its rocks.
The burning moon won't fizzle and fade
before the midnight's children take
leave of their nocturnal tenements
and roam the streets devoid
of names.

Sweet misery, the hours won't
consume the lonely little seconds
the way a man's palms devour
his tears. The white curtains by
the windows won't salvage an ardor
spent hidden in a room it has sheltered
for many years.

Sweet misery, the rain won't
trickle tenderly from the heavens
long before our hands can shield
our eyes. The days and nights won't
go by long before we've survived
a lost love's unending goodbyes.

Standing Alone Outside in the Obsidian of Night

The wind sweeps you in.

You're at the center of your backyard seemingly

in the center of everything. Where

the barren trees once eerily

cradled a slice

of the sun, a faint phosphorescent glow

now shimmers into

the horizon.

The moon hides in the dark opulence

of the clouds. You stare high

up into the sky and a gust

of wind draws

you in once more,

encircling, dancing low

before rising into the hazy

afterglow above.

You feel faint with your own shimmering,

the world of the opaque within you

rustling with the quiet

notion that you stand

in the midst of something greater than the mere

quotidian of understanding.

Everything is in the now,

and everything is in the imminent.

Everything is falling.

Everything is rising.

Does She Dance?

Tell me, Montpelier.
Do the clouds above harbor
any chance? Does
the green, green grass

relish the ardor?
Does she dance? Does
she dance? So, does she?
Does she waltz

to the melody of a midnight's
symphony of romance?
Empty cellars aplenty,
mountains of ash.

So tell me, friend, does she
not or does she? Do
roaming eyes affix themselves
in a trance? Does

she dance? Does she
Dance? Do cold, callous hands
rekindle the ensuing
reverie? Do the walls

within your manse

swoon upon the dance?

So, does she? In the night?

or in the day? In

whatever trepidations lay?

Tell me, Montpelier.

Does she dance? Does she

dance? Does she?

Nineveh

Ah, what span of time finds you gone?
At what direction finds the sun fading to grey
in the cold winds of a storm, oh Nineveh?
What celestial season may last as long?

Ah, what nomad of the vast desert sand
calls you home? What capricious fate awaits
a man who lays his tired bones in the bulk
of another's frail remains, oh Nineveh?
Does your denizen know no shame?

Ah, what unearthly desire spurs your women
to tread upon and slowly sink beneath the mire?
What willowy ways draw voyagers far
and away at the mere utterance of your name,
oh Nineveh? Do the fallen fray freely
enter and within your walls remain?

Ah, what insalubrious soul finds you
in foremost control? What pales in taste
to Nebuchadnezzar's gates is any one
of your own, oh Nineveh? Do your truant
walls hear ruin with the winds of change?

Darkly

Why does stardust sparkle across the westerly winds?

I don't know why.

A faint shimmer emerges from the northern mists.

A fire spreads beneath the Sahara sun.

Throngs of the populace flood the city streets.

Strangers, regardless, they meet.

At the turn of the tide, less come into the black wings of the
night.

Cloves of fire mark the ancient sky.

Why does the slow tide ravage the sands of time?

I don't know why.

It is only this thin veil of a dream I spur into belief.

That the ensuing darkness will dissipate into the light.

Stigmata

I am half the man I used to be. Half
the shadow that I was. Half
the beating heart in its barren husk.
Yet, even then I measured up
to very little of what should've been.
And now all is lost.

I am half the patch of darkness within. Half
the parody and its matching paroxysm. Half
the brooding mind and its nomenclature
of sun, moon, earth, and sky. Yet
I would have it better if I could leave it
all behind. At whatever the cost.

I am half the ocean's tide in the rippling sea. Half
the humming that spurs the melody. Half
the finite dream on the fringes of eternity.
Yet, the world spans so little and turns
less and less at the great prognosticator's
expense. I would so much as dream the devil
were to beware. If I so dare.

Music For Airports

Life transcends. Life begins anew.

The mantra never ends. The waves of wonderment

never cease. We rehearse a full repertoire

of comings and goings. Who amongst us

has yet to leave?

Time is not a constant. It expires. It

renews vigor in but a second. Splendor

with but a blink of an eye.

Rapture in but a moment. It is required no further

announcement

upon its audience. Who amongst us

has yet to arrive?

The winds have no genesis. Windows

And stairwells share an obvious difference.

Hellos mark the incipience. Departures succeed farewells.

Empty chairs and tables are each

an antithesis. They mainly bear witness.

They devolve such

occurrences.

Continuity leads to stagnation;

Stagnation leads to continuity.

Everything shifts. Everything changes. Nothing is wasted.

The infinite takes place even in the stillness.

Thoughts shoot off in different

directions. The heart runs through

the gamut of emotions.

Sleep

To want. To crave. The rapture of resting

one's limbs amiably

in the shade.

The hope of a bottle cast upon the pitiless

wave. The journey ends

where it begins.

The amnesty of sleep.

A raft forsaken to the sea of escape.

A summer's dream mourns the turn

of the fall.

Or else, nothing at all,

and suddenly

one finds himself awake.

This Fire

The heart is unaware, oh

do not despair.

It knows only its breadth of wanting;

The waves of wallowing at the peak of its torrent.

That the breadth of its torment may at once

be transient, that in itself, is its own

deterrent. To say that such

a rekindling is sparked

and at once flourishes unto its own fulfilling,

that such an intangible art

may, from its incipience, never

depart, that this palpable heart dreams

of its anguish as it does its

own inevitable undoing.

Ah, do not despair

the volition so unaware

of its own doom foretelling.

Is it not despair's dominion that binds

us to our descent into the depths of oblivion?

And such a prospect as this oblivion not

therefore catapult us into the depths of despair?

That we are borne of the earth, and our souls fashioned

from the breath of fire, that we are thus one
with the light which in turn is life itself,
and one with the inundations of desire.
For whatever it is within us that we so truly
covet. Whatever it is within the clouds above
that conceal the sky or the volatile fires
below it.

I am Unloved

I have come and I have gone…I am one.
To my distinction I have beguiled my sullen art,
the temple and the tomb…the years span the
trenches of the heart. I loved sooner than I thought…
the veil never lifted on disbelief suspended.
The evening dress drifts in the invisible air
Of insurmountable bliss…the doves are silent…
the tempest is at its peak of torment.
I long for your kiss…all efforts are fruitless.
> I am unloved.

The questions remain untouched…the answers
remain unrevealed…who am I?
Wanton indiscernible passer-by? Vagabond
on borrowed time? My lips are sealed.
Reality is its severed seal. I hear whispers
in the dark…the flowers blossom your unmistakable
air wherever you are…the nights are heralds
to the sun…but I find you gone.
> I am unloved.

Such is the world…pinnacles of dust are all
of what we see and touch. It is only unto death
will life bequeath its warmth. All flesh
is but a fury driven, and the rivers flowing

without their fervor roll forever unforgiven.

We fathom what we are worth…I have none.

       I am unloved.

I have come and I have gone. I am one.

The pillars are begotten of strength.

The darkness is the irredeemable sun. Your elation

is my corporeal desperation. The candles burn.

The moon drifts in a fog beyond earth.

The gravedigger digs his dirt.

The undertaker sings his song…you have gone…

but not above.

       I am unloved.

Obsecration to Death

I fear I am in love with death.

Death in a child's rocking chair swinging

to its own accompaniment in the summer's

molten air.

Death in an old lamp

sporadically called upon to light an old room

half a century left forgotten to drown

in fits of despair and forlorn, foretelling doom.

Death in a brush of auburn leaves

twisting high in the autumn breeze nevermore

to see the branches onto which they

were borne with the purpose of living

in a world of trees.

If death were forlorn

love in a theoretical sort of way…forgotten,

abandoned, misspent, would I love

a woman's hairbrush and the beautiful way

in which it was once used. Or taking to

an old café in Stalingrad by train. Or crossing

an old bridge in Deep Run like I used

to in times when I sought solace from

the vagaries of a summer's day. If death were in

retrospect a shred of life once lived nevermore

to once again be revisited, might I touch

the prison of existence in such an object and

re-experience it, if only to therefore

defeat such a death? Or am I merely taken

by it, smitten by the ardor of abandonment

so much so that each attempt to foreshadow an

ending with the haunting semblance of

meaning is really like a purloined letter

penned to one's betrothed?

To be one who is

in love with the memory of an event. To relish life

the way it was once lived. To console lamentation

with the memory of each moment.

To hasten the disinterment of a seemingly

impenetrable omen.

And so, I fear I am in love

with death.

Death in the austere features

of a ruined man's face and his most private

and solitary of erstwhile ruined convictions.

Death in the last page of

a day-by-day desk calendar bestowed upon by

a good friend with the most touching of modest intentions
one of which is to remind oneself to live
life to the fullest.

Death in an art exhibition's rendition
of the burning bush and its lore, with the devouring fire
snaking up higher and higher up the arms
of a twisting sycamore.

All That Remains

From what once was

there is now nothing else.

Nothing beneath the harsh white light.

Nothing in the sound of the cold steel bed

wheeling into the heart of darkness.

But what of darkness regained

is darkness bereft? Isn't darkness

meant to be the absence of light?

The heart is different.

The heart tells the mind what is best for it.

the lulling of an old song,

the drubbing of an old desire.

It starts very slow and then it rages

through the house of cards

like a fire.

When the heart only tells the mind

its unfulfilled passions, it

remembers everything

forlorn, forsaken.

It seeks only to unearth the remains

of an old stigmata in its grave

deep inside.

When all else fails, all else fall prey

to the frailty of the flesh, one clings

desperately to all that remains.

The harsh white light,

the invisible words of a blank page,

the dark womb of night.

Aftermath

Most idyllic fantasies of mine are set to stars.

The night's caresses are soft and intimate.

When the architecture of the will is steady as the wind.

The heart is pliant as the vine.

Lately, the mornings have been polluted with the enigmatic.

The dire dialectics of a night's dreaming in the wake

of its opulent language.

I awaken with a rustling of the senses.

I awaken each day with the realization that I expect

some idea of happiness to come in the form

of someone, something, or a lot of these

at once, though I am aware

that they may never come

or that if they do come at all

that happiness may not come with them.

The bare objects of the room seem to grimly acknowledge.

They seem to be waiting for something to come,

Something that is already happening.

Each is like a tombstone awash with light.

Cold, bare, aware of the infinitesimal.

They wait for the coming

of the night.

Printed in the United States
129636LV00004B/13/P